Welcome to Ultimate Family Puzzles NUMBERS

All the family can enjoy Ultimate Family Puzzles: numbers as it has something to suit everyone. It contains popular puzzles such as Sudoku, Kakuro, number Sequences, Magic Squares and many more.

There are three levels of difficulty in this book. easy puzzles are marked with one star and, as the name suggests, are the most simple puzzles to do. These are suitable for the youngest child or the puzzle beginner. the moderate puzzles are that little bit harder, and have been highlighted with two stars for those who feel that the easy puzzles do not provide enough of a challenge.

Then finally there are the challenging puzzles, which are marked with three stars. These are for serious puzzlers only and represnt the peak of difficulty. So, sometihng for ll the family to sit down together and enjoy!

EASY ⭐

MODERATE ⭐⭐

CHALLENGING ⭐⭐⭐

igloo

Published in 2007
by Igloo Books Ltd
Cottage Farm,
Sywell,
NN6 0BJ.
www.igloo-books.com

© Igloo Books Ltd 2006

ISBN: 978-1-84561-517-8

Printed in China.

DOMINO PLACEMENT

A standard set of dominoes has been laid out, using only the dominoes shown below each puzzle. Can you draw in the edges of them all? The check-box is provided as an aid, and in some puzzles, a starting domino has been placed, which will get you on your way.

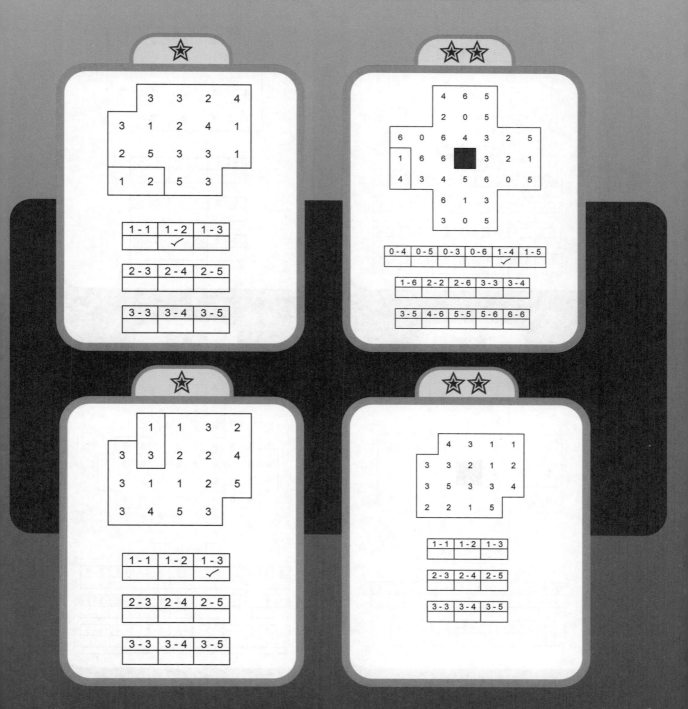

Puzzle 1 (★):

3	3	2	4
3	1	2	4	1
2	5	3	3	1
1	2	5	3

1 - 1	1 - 2	1 - 3
	✓	

2 - 3	2 - 4	2 - 5

3 - 3	3 - 4	3 - 5

Puzzle 2 (★★):

		4	6	5		
		2	0	5		
6	0	6	4	3	2	5
1	6	6	■	3	2	1
4	3	4	5	6	0	5
		6	1	3		
		3	0	5		

0 - 4	0 - 5	0 - 3	0 - 6	1 - 4	1 - 5
				✓	

1 - 6	2 - 2	2 - 6	3 - 3	3 - 4

3 - 5	4 - 6	5 - 5	5 - 6	6 - 6

Puzzle 3 (★):

	1	1	3	2
3	3	2	2	4
3	1	1	2	5
3	4	5	3

1 - 1	1 - 2	1 - 3
		✓

2 - 3	2 - 4	2 - 5

3 - 3	3 - 4	3 - 5

Puzzle 4 (★★):

	4	3	1	1
3	3	2	1	2
3	5	3	3	4
2	2	1	5

1 - 1	1 - 2	1 - 3

2 - 3	2 - 4	2 - 5

3 - 3	3 - 4	3 - 5

Turn to page 54 for the solutions **3**

DOMINO PLACEMENT

★★★

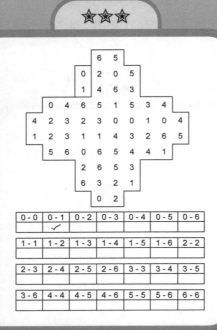

0 - 0	0 - 1	0 - 2	0 - 3	0 - 4	0 - 5	0 - 6
	✓					

1 - 1	1 - 2	1 - 3	1 - 4	1 - 5	1 - 6	2 - 2

2 - 3	2 - 4	2 - 5	2 - 6	3 - 3	3 - 4	3 - 5

3 - 6	4 - 4	4 - 5	4 - 6	5 - 5	5 - 6	6 - 6

★

2	5	2	3
2	1	1	5	3
4	4	3	1	2
1	3	3	3

1 - 1	1 - 2	1 - 3

2 - 3	2 - 4	2 - 5

3 - 3	3 - 4	3 - 5

★★

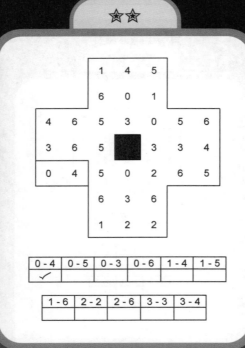

0 - 4	0 - 5	0 - 3	0 - 6	1 - 4	1 - 5
✓					

1 - 6	2 - 2	2 - 6	3 - 3	3 - 4

★★★

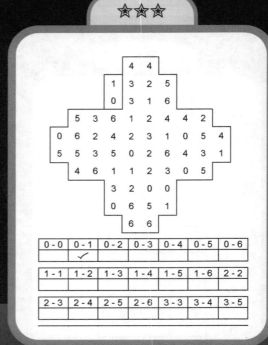

0 - 0	0 - 1	0 - 2	0 - 3	0 - 4	0 - 5	0 - 6
	✓					

1 - 1	1 - 2	1 - 3	1 - 4	1 - 5	1 - 6	2 - 2

2 - 3	2 - 4	2 - 5	2 - 6	3 - 3	3 - 4	3 - 5

DOMINO PLACEMENT

A standard set of dominoes has been laid out, using only the dominoes shown below each puzzle. Can you draw in the edges of them all? The check-box is provided as an aid, and in some puzzles, a starting domino has been placed, which will get you on your way.

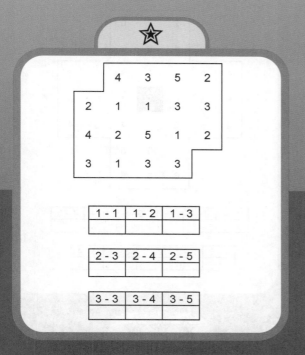

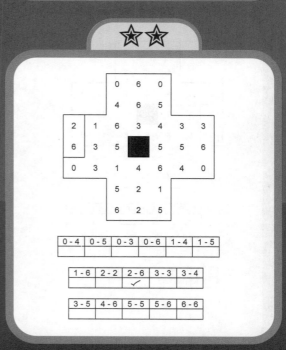

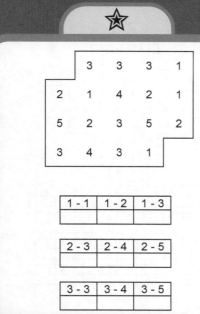

Turn to page 54 for the solutions **5**

DOMINO PLACEMENT

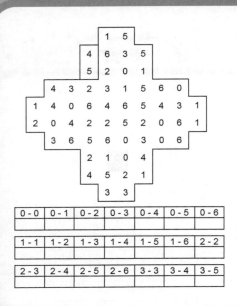

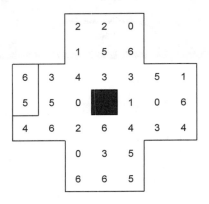

0-0	0-1	0-2	0-3	0-4	0-5	0-6

1-1	1-2	1-3	1-4	1-5	1-6	2-2

2-3	2-4	2-5	2-6	3-3	3-4	3-5

0-4	0-5	0-3	0-6	1-4	1-5

1-6	2-2	2-6	3-3	3-4

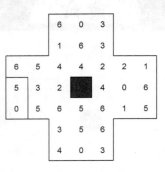

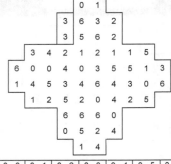

0-4	0-5	0-3	0-6	1-4	1-5
	✓				

1-6	2-2	2-6	3-3	3-4

3-5	4-6	5-5	5-6	6-6

0-0	0-1	0-2	0-3	0-4	0-5	0-6

1-1	1-2	1-3	1-4	1-5	1-6	2-2

2-3	2-4	2-5	2-6	3-3	3-4	3-5
				✓		

3-6	4-4	4-5	4-6	5-5	5-6	6-6

DOMINO PLACEMENT

A standard set of dominoes has been laid out, using only the dominoes shown below each puzzle. Can you draw in the edges of them all? The check-box is provided as an aid, and in some puzzles, a starting domino has been placed, which will get you on your way.

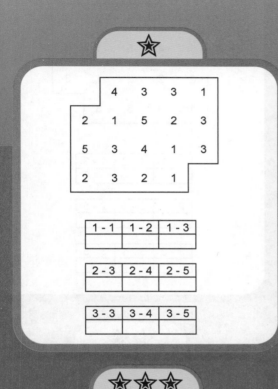

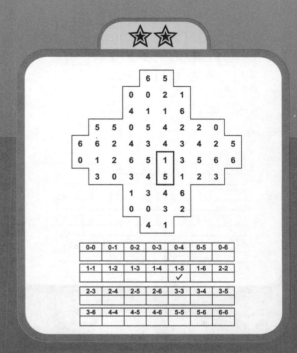

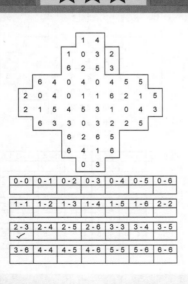

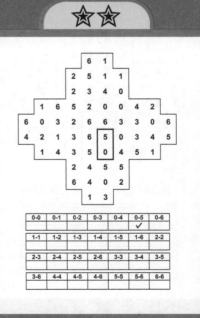

DOMINO PLACEMENT

 ★★★

```
        5 1
      6 3 2 3
      5 4 1 0
  4 6 0 4 5 3 1 2
2 0 4 5 4 6 0 5 4 3
6 1 3 0 0 6 2 5 6 0
  2 5 2 4 1 1 3 3
      6 5 6 2
      1 3 0 2
      4 1
```

0 - 0	0 - 1	0 - 2	0 - 3	0 - 4	0 - 5	0 - 6

1 - 1	1 - 2	1 - 3	1 - 4	1 - 5	1 - 6	2 - 2

2 - 3	2 - 4	2 - 5	2 - 6	3 - 3	3 - 4	3 - 5
✓						

3 - 6	4 - 4	4 - 5	4 - 6	5 - 5	5 - 6	6 - 6

 ★

```
    3 3 2 3
1 4 5 1 4
2 2 2 1 3
1 3 5 3
```

1 - 1	1 - 2	1 - 3

2 - 3	2 - 4	2 - 5

3 - 3	3 - 4	3 - 5

★★

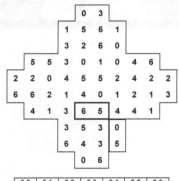

```
      0 3
    1 5 6 1
    3 2 6 0
5 5 3 0 1 0 4 6
2 2 0 4 5 5 2 4 2 2
6 6 2 1 4 0 1 2 1 3
  4 1 3 6 5 4 4 1
      3 5 3 0
      6 4 3 5
        0 6
```

0-0	0-1	0-2	0-3	0-4	0-5	0-6
					✓	

1-1	1-2	1-3	1-4	1-5	1-6	2-2

2-3	2-4	2-5	2-6	3-3	3-4	3-5

3-6	4-4	4-5	4-6	5-5	5-6	6-6
					✓	

★★

```
        2 6
      5 2 3 5
      1 5 1 2
  6 0 2 4 0 5 3 4
1 5 3 4 1 1 5 1 2 6
4 2 0 6 2 4 4 5 4 6
3 0 4 0 6 0 6 0
      0 3 2 3
      5 3 6 1
        1 3
```

0 - 0	0 - 1	0 - 2	0 - 3	0 - 4	0 - 5	0 - 6

1 - 1	1 - 2	1 - 3	1 - 4	1 - 5	1 - 6	2 - 2
✓						

2 - 3	2 - 4	2 - 5	2 - 6	3 - 3	3 - 4	3 - 5

3 - 6	4 - 4	4 - 5	4 - 6	5 - 5	5 - 6	6 - 6

DOMINO PLACEMENT

A standard set of dominoes has been laid out, using only the dominoes shown below each puzzle. Can you draw in the edges of them all? The check-box is provided as an aid, and in some puzzles, a starting domino has been placed, which will get you on your way.

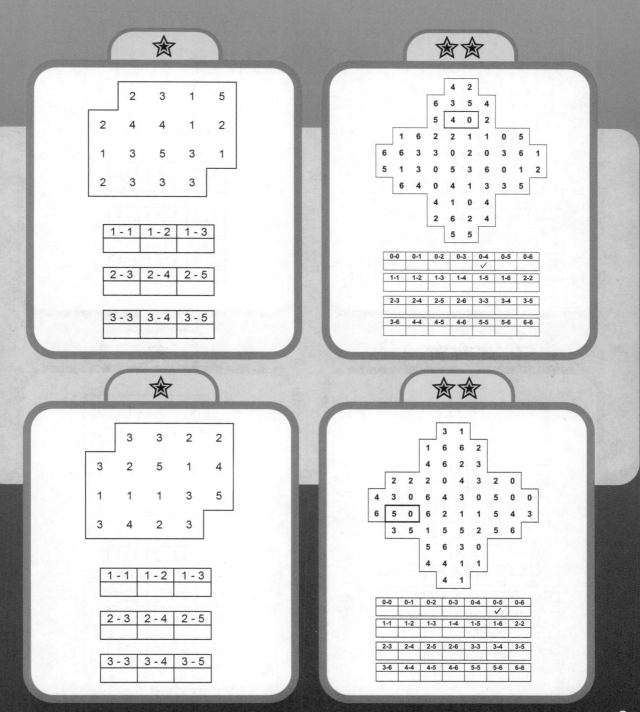

Turn to page 55 for the solutions **9**

DOMINO PLACEMENT

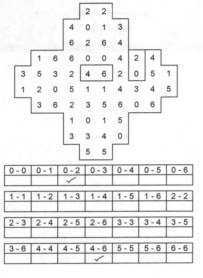

```
        2 2
      4 0 1 3
      6 2 6 4
  1 6 6 0 0 4 2 4
3 5 3 2 4 6 2 0 5 1
1 2 0 5 1 1 4 3 4 5
  3 6 2 3 5 6 0 6
        1 0 1 5
        3 3 4 0
          5 5
```

0 - 0	0 - 1	0 - 2	0 - 3	0 - 4	0 - 5	0 - 6
		✓				

1 - 1	1 - 2	1 - 3	1 - 4	1 - 5	1 - 6	2 - 2

2 - 3	2 - 4	2 - 5	2 - 6	3 - 3	3 - 4	3 - 5

3 - 6	4 - 4	4 - 5	4 - 6	5 - 5	5 - 6	6 - 6
			✓			

```
          2 1 2 5
  2 4 3 3     1
  3 1 4 5     3
  3 1 3 2
```

1 - 1	1 - 2	1 - 3
		✓

2 - 3	2 - 4	2 - 5

3 - 3	3 - 4	3 - 5

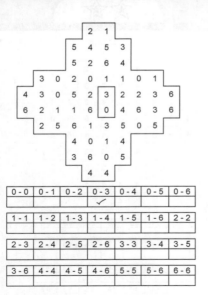

```
        2 1
      5 4 5 3
      5 2 6 4
    3 0 2 0 1 1 0 1
  4 3 0 5 2 3 2 2 3 6
  6 2 1 1 6 0 4 6 3 6
    2 5 6 1 3 5 0 5
        4 0 1 4
        3 6 0 5
          4 4
```

0 - 0	0 - 1	0 - 2	0 - 3	0 - 4	0 - 5	0 - 6
			✓			

1 - 1	1 - 2	1 - 3	1 - 4	1 - 5	1 - 6	2 - 2

2 - 3	2 - 4	2 - 5	2 - 6	3 - 3	3 - 4	3 - 5

3 - 6	4 - 4	4 - 5	4 - 6	5 - 5	5 - 6	6 - 6

```
    4 3 1 1
  3 3 2 1 2
  3 5 3 3 4
  2 2 1 5
```

1 - 1	1 - 2	1 - 3

2 - 3	2 - 4	2 - 5

3 - 3	3 - 4	3 - 5

DOMINO PLACEMENT

A standard set of dominoes has been laid out, using only the dominoes shown below each puzzle. Can you draw in the edges of them all? The check-box is provided as an aid, and in some puzzles, a starting domino has been placed, which will get you on your way.

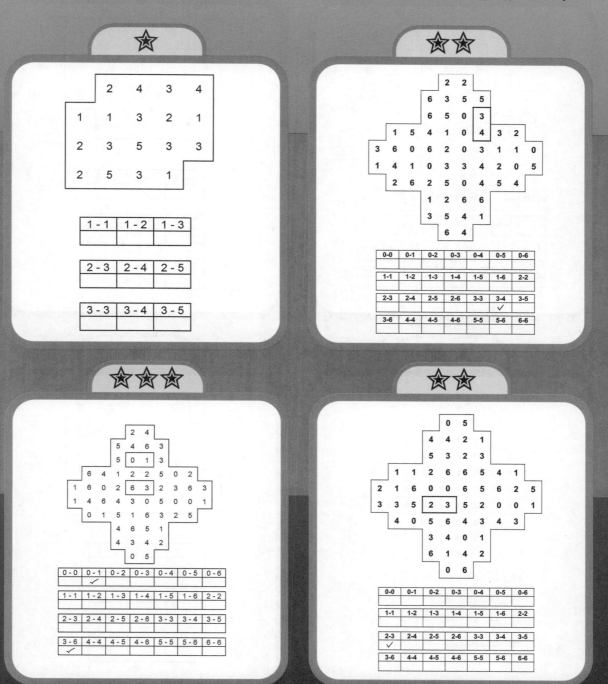

Turn to page 55 for the solutions **11**

DOMINO PLACEMENT

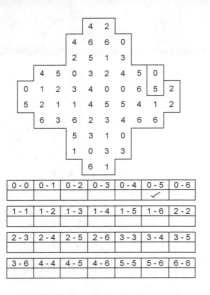

0 - 0	0 - 1	0 - 2	0 - 3	0 - 4	0 - 5 ✓	0 - 6

1 - 1	1 - 2	1 - 3	1 - 4	1 - 5	1 - 6	2 - 2

2 - 3	2 - 4	2 - 5	2 - 6	3 - 3	3 - 4	3 - 5

3 - 6	4 - 4	4 - 5	4 - 6	5 - 5	5 - 6	6 - 6

```
        4 3 2 5
    2 3 1 3 5
    1 3 2 1 3
    2 4 3 1
```

1 - 1	1 - 2	1 - 3

2 - 3	2 - 4	2 - 5

3 - 3	3 - 4	3 - 5

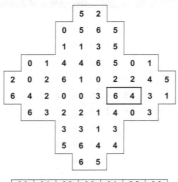

0-0	0-1	0-2	0-3	0-4	0-5	0-6

1-1	1-2	1-3	1-4	1-5	1-6	2-2

2-3	2-4	2-5	2-6	3-3	3-4	3-5

3-6	4-4	4-5	4-6	5-5	5-6	6-6
			✓			

```
      2 5 2 3
  2 1 2 4 3
  3 3 3 1 4
  1 1 3 5
```

1 - 1	1 - 2	1 - 3

2 - 3	2 - 4	2 - 5

3 - 3	3 - 4	3 - 5

KAKURO

In Kakuro the numbers in the black squares refer to the SUMS of the digits which you are to fill into the empty spaces. The number ABOVE the diagonal line refers to the empty spaces directly to the RIGHT of that number. A number BELOW the diagonal line refers to the empty spaces directly BELOW that number. No zeros are used here and a digit can only appear once in any particular digit combination.

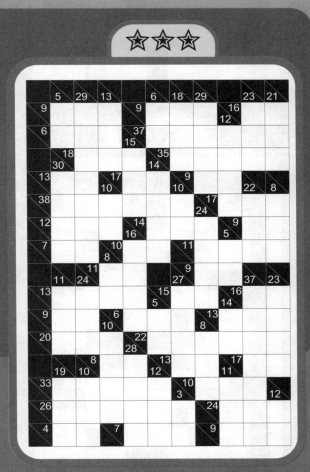

Turn to page 56 for the solutions **13**

KAKURO

In Kakuro the numbers in the black squares refer to the SUMS of the digits which you are to fill into the empty spaces. The number ABOVE the diagonal line refers to the empty spaces directly to the RIGHT of that number. A number BELOW the diagonal line refers to the empty spaces directly BELOW that number. No zeros are used here and a digit can only appear once in any particular digit combination.

Turn to page 56 for the solutions **15**

KAKURO

KAKURO

In Kakuro the numbers in the black squares refer to the SUMS of the digits which you are to fill into the empty spaces. The number ABOVE the diagonal line refers to the empty spaces directly to the RIGHT of that number. A number BELOW the diagonal line refers to the empty spaces directly BELOW that number. No zeros are used here and a digit can only appear once in any particular digit combination.

Turn to page 56 for the solutions

KAKURO

KAKURO

In Kakuro the numbers in the black squares refer to the SUMS of the digits which you are to fill into the empty spaces. The number ABOVE the diagonal line refers to the empty spaces directly to the RIGHT of that number. A number BELOW the diagonal line refers to the empty spaces directly BELOW that number. No zeros are used here and a digit can only appear once in any particular digit combination.

KAKURO

KAKURO

In Kakuro the numbers in the black squares refer to the SUMS of the digits which you are to fill into the empty spaces. The number ABOVE the diagonal line refers to the empty spaces directly to the RIGHT of that number. A number BELOW the diagonal line refers to the empty spaces directly BELOW that number. No zeros are used here and a digit can only appear once in any particular digit combination.

Turn to page 57 for the solutions

KAKURO

WHATEVER NEXT?

★★

20	18
14	12

31	16
8	9

18	16
15	15

?

A

16	11
31	20

B

9	22
18	15

C

17	19
18	15

★

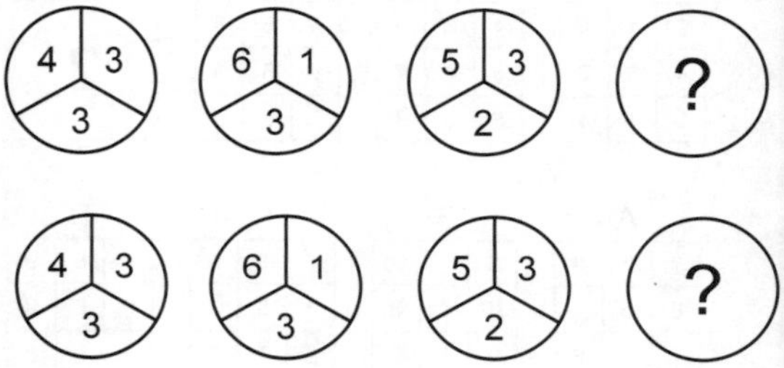

Which of the three circles below fits most logically into the empty circle above?

★★

13	17
9	13

18	13
11	6

5	8
7	10

?

Which of the three squares below fits most logically into the empty square above?

A

8	10
11	13

B

12	9
8	13

C

14	9
11	13

★

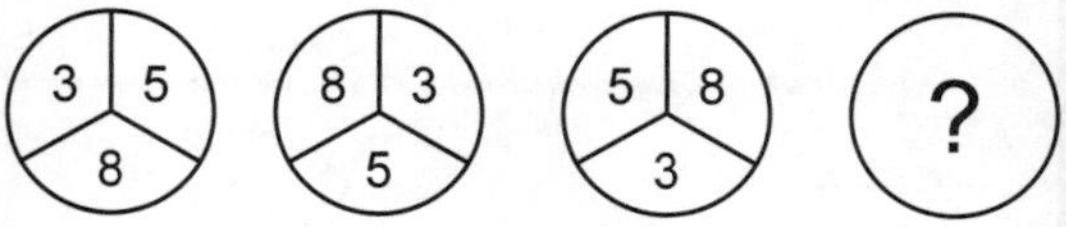

Which of the three circles below fits most logically into the empty circle above?

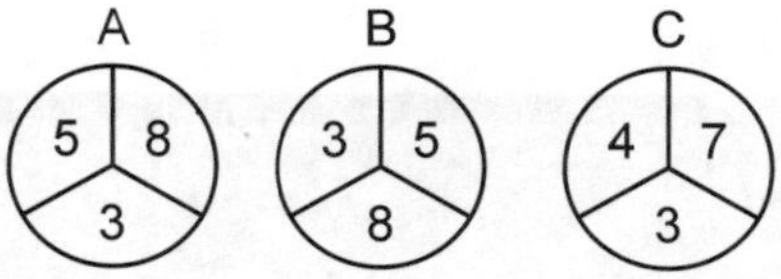

Turn to page 57 for the solutions

WHATEVER NEXT?

★★★

2	1	4
4	3	2
3	1	1

4	3	6
6	4	4
5	3	3

6	5	8
8	5	6
7	5	5

?

A

7	7	9
8	5	7
7	6	6

B

8	7	10
10	6	8
9	7	7

C

7	8	9
8	5	7
9	7	7

D

7	8	9
9	6	8
7	6	6

★★

5	2
2	5

5	4
5	1

10	2
1	5

?

Which of the three squares below fits most logically into the empty square above?

A

5	8
2	2

B

8	7
2	1

C

1	5
20	1

★★

5	4
7	3

6	6
11	6

7	8
15	9

?

Which of the three squares below fits most logically into the empty square above?

A

9	11
18	15

B

8	10
19	12

C

11	10
8	16

★★★

8	1	3
3	6	6
7	4	7

6	2	4
8	3	4
6	6	6

5	6	1
6	5	4
4	9	5

?

Which of the four squares below fits most logically into the empty square above

A

7	3	2
7	4	4
6	7	5

B

8	1	2
6	4	9
6	6	6

C

6	4	2
8	3	6
7	6	5

D

7	2	3
4	7	4
6	8	7

9	8
7	10

11	13
8	16

15	11
19	7

?

Which of the three squares below fits most logically into the empty square above?

A

8	7
10	9

B

12	6
4	10

C

12	6
13	5

Which of the three circles below fits most logically into the empty circle above?

A   B   C

8	29
15	22

17	38
24	31

4	25
11	18

?

Which of the three squares below fits most logically into the empty square above?

A

11	31
20	26

B

19	40
26	33

C

7	19
9	11

Which of the three circles below fits most logically into the empty circle above?

A   B   C

Turn to page 58 for the solutions **25**

WHATEVER NEXT?

Puzzle 1 ★★★

11	8	7
5	3	6
14	12	9

22	4	14
10	6	3
7	6	18

11	2	7
5	3	6
14	3	9

?

Which of the four squares below fits most logically into the empty square above

A

11	4	7
10	3	6
6	7	18

B

22	8	14
5	6	6
7	6	9

C

22	1	14
10	6	3
7	6	18

D

22	1	14
5	3	3
7	3	18

Puzzle 2 ★

Circle 1: 8 | 8 / 9
Circle 2: 8 | 7 / 10
Circle 3: 6 | 11 / 8
Circle 4: ?

Which of the three circles below fits most logically into the empty circle above?

A: 12 | 6 / 7
B: 8 | 6 / 9
C: 11 | 7 / 9

Puzzle 3 ★★

17	26
8	62

161	17
71	8

35	116
206	44

?

Which of the three squares below fits most logically into the empty square above?

A

8	62
71	26

B

26	36
7	19

C

181	27
9	62

Puzzle 4 ★★★

9	11	10
4	5	3
6	7	5

8	3	5
2	3	1
4	2	4

9	10	9
3	5	6
7	4	3

?

Which of the four squares below fits most logically into the empty square above

A

13	12	15
16	6	2
9	3	4

B

9	7	8
4	3	9
6	4	3

C

5	9	2
1	2	2
8	6	4

D

3	12	7
6	3	7
8	7	4

4	3
12	5

8	16
6	2

3	11
4	4

?

Which of the three squares below fits most logically into the empty square above?

A

13	8
3	2

B

15	8
4	6

C

6	3
7	14

Circles: 1 | 3 / 4 · 6 | 8 / 9 · 11 | 13 / 14 · ?

Which of the three circles below fits most logically into the empty circle above?

A 18 | 16 / 13 **B** 12 | 7 / 9 **C** 16 | 18 / 19

6		
		4
	3	

		6
4		
	3	

3		4
		6

?

Which of the four squares below fits most logically into the empty square above

A

4		
		6
	3	

B

6		
		4
	3	

C

3		
4		
6		

D

3		6
	4	

Circles: 16 | 8 / 12 · 4 | 12 / 20 · 20 | 16 / 8 · ?

Which of the three circles below fits most logically into the empty circle above?

A 14 | 7 / 9 **B** 8 | 20 / 12 **C** 6 | 12 / 18

WHATEVER NEXT?

★★★

3	12	2
16	4	8
4	12	3

2	6	1
9	3	3
3	15	5

6	30	7
20	5	35
4	15	3

?

Which of the four squares below fits most logically into the empty square above

A

4	19	7
12	4	18
6	15	3

B

8	20	9
13	3	18
5	16	4

C

4	20	6
25	5	35
7	25	9

D

9	18	6
10	2	12
5	14	7

★★

13	8
1	20

22	17
10	29

31	26
19	38

?

Which of the three squares below fits most logically into the empty square above?

A

20	33
26	41

B

36	40
26	18

C

40	35
28	47

★★

4	2
40	5

6	2
48	4

5	2
60	6

?

Which of the three squares below fits most logically into the empty square above?

A

3	7
29	4

B

3	5
45	3

C

6	2
38	4

★★★

8	2	7
9	4	8
9	4	8

3	2	7
9	6	8
7	4	11

11	2	7
9	5	8
8	4	4

?

Which of the four squares below fits most logically into the empty square above

A

7	2	4
9	8	8
8	4	5

B

7	2	3
9	6	8
8	4	4

C

2	2	7
9	9	8
4	4	6

D

4	2	6
9	7	8
8	4	4

Puzzle 1

6	12
3	24

14	28
7	56

12	24
6	48

?

Which of the three squares below fits most logically into the empty square above?

A

8	16
4	32

B

5	10
3	18

C

18	24
9	38

Puzzle 2

Which of the three circles below fits most logically into the empty circle above?

A   B   C

Puzzle 3

1	2
3	4

1	4
12	12

1	8
48	36

?

Which of the three squares below fits most logically into the empty square above?

A

2	16
64	50

B

1	12
64	48

C

1	16
192	108

Puzzle 4

Which of the three circles below fits most logically into the empty circle above?

A   B   C

Turn to page 58 for the solutions **29**

⭐⭐⭐

7	8	9
4	3	6
3	5	3

6	4	5
4	1	3
2	3	2

7	9	8
6	4	7
1	5	1

?

Which of the four squares below fits most logically into the empty square above

A

6	8	9
4	5	6
3	4	4

B

6	4	8
4	2	7
4	3	2

C

8	4	7
7	3	8
2	1	1

D

6	3	2
4	1	2
2	2	0

⭐⭐

7	6
4	9

6	9
7	4

9	4
6	7

?

Which of the three squares below fits most logically into the empty square above?

A

4	7
9	6

B

9	7
4	6

C

6	7
9	4

⭐⭐

4	6
9	6

8	4
6	12

6	8
4	3

?

Which of the three squares below fits most logically into the empty square above?

A

8	6
7	7

B

20	4
3	15

C

9	5
3	8

⭐⭐⭐

4	5	3
2	6	7
4	9	8

4	2	4
9	6	5
8	7	3

8	9	4
7	6	2
3	5	4

?

Which of the four squares below fits most logically into the empty square above

A

3	7	8
8	6	4
7	4	2

B

3	7	8
5	5	9
2	4	4

C

5	3	7
4	6	8
2	4	9

D

3	7	8
5	6	9
4	2	4

⭐⭐

3	4
4	4

7	6
9	8

11	13
10	11

?

Which of the three squares below fits most logically into the empty square above?

A

13	14
20	8

B

12	10
8	11

C

17	18
10	15

⭐

Which of the three circles below fits most logically into the empty circle above?

A **B** **C**

⭐⭐

3	16
14	2

14	3
1	10

25	2
5	17

?

Which of the three squares below fits most logically into the empty square above?

A

10	18
25	3

B

9	34
38	3

C

8	21
60	4

⭐

Which of the three circles below fits most logically into the empty circle above?

A **B** **C**

5	4	5
7	3	2
5	4	5

4	5	3
4	1	2
5	4	4

6	5	8
6	3	4
7	7	4

?

Which of the four squares below fits most logically into the empty square above

A

7	8	8
6	4	6
6	5	4

B

6	8	7
2	3	4
4	3	3

C

8	6	3
9	4	7
2	6	4

D

9	6	2
7	4	3
1		

12	20	11
19	15	14
16	12	22

18	6	19
13	26	20
16	15	8

17	15	14
19	19	16
11	13	17

?

Which of the four squares below fits most logically into the empty space above?

A

17	23	15
18	13	18
11	11	14

B

17	23	15
19	13	18
11	11	14

C

17	22	15
19	13	18
11	11	14

D

17	23	15
19	13	18
14	11	14

Which figure below continues the sequence above?

10	10	3
28	2	27
20	26	12

50	47	43
41	5	52
4	5	58

6	17	78
68	61	7
16	70	73

?

Which of the four squares below fits most logically into the empty square above

A

6	66	7
61	8	76
16	68	60

B

77	68	87
7	17	17
18	70	72

C

9	96	9
92	19	19
91	99	97

D

5	60	40
56	4	55
42	66	5

COMBIKU

Each horizontal row and vertical column should contain different colors and different numbers. Every square will contain one number and one colored circle and no combination may be repeated anywhere in the puzzle; so, for instance, if a square contains a 3 surrounded by a red circle, then no other square containing a 3 will have a red circle and no other square with a red circle will contain a 3.

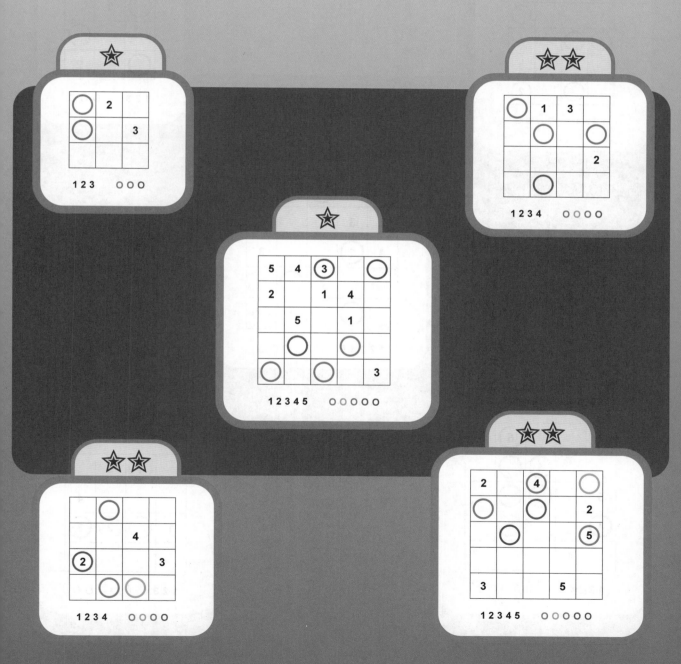

Turn to page 59 for the solutions 33

★

1234 ○○○○

★

123 ○○○

★

12345 ○○○○○

★★

12345 ○○○○○

★

1234 ○○○○

COMBIKU

Each horizontal row and vertical column should contain different colors and different numbers. Every square will contain one number and one colored circle and no combination may be repeated anywhere in the puzzle; so, for instance, if a square contains a 3 surrounded by a red circle, then no other square containing a 3 will have a red circle and no other square with a red circle will contain a 3.

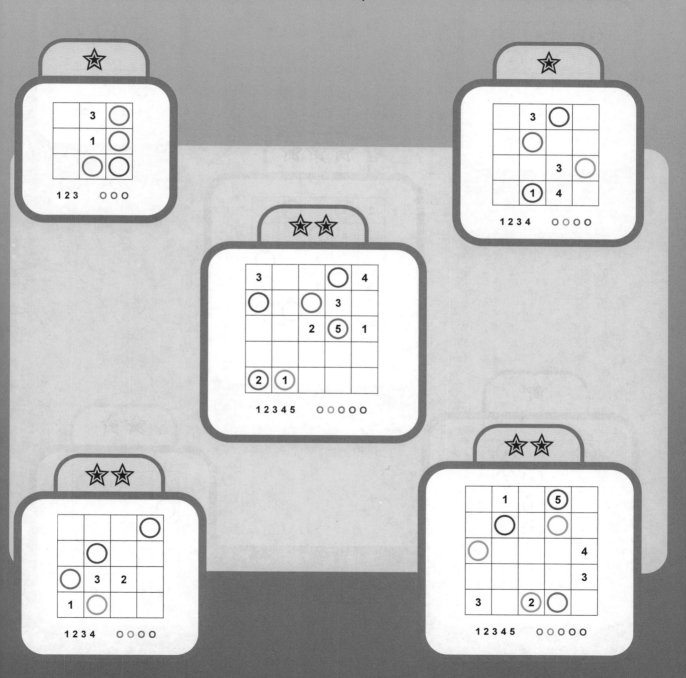

Turn to page 60 for the solutions

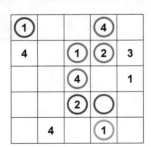

COMBIKU

Each horizontal row and vertical column should contain different colors and different numbers. Every square will contain one number and one colored circle and no combination may be repeated anywhere in the puzzle; so, for instance, if a square contains a 3 surrounded by a red circle, then no other square containing a 3 will have a red circle and no other square with a red circle will contain a 3.

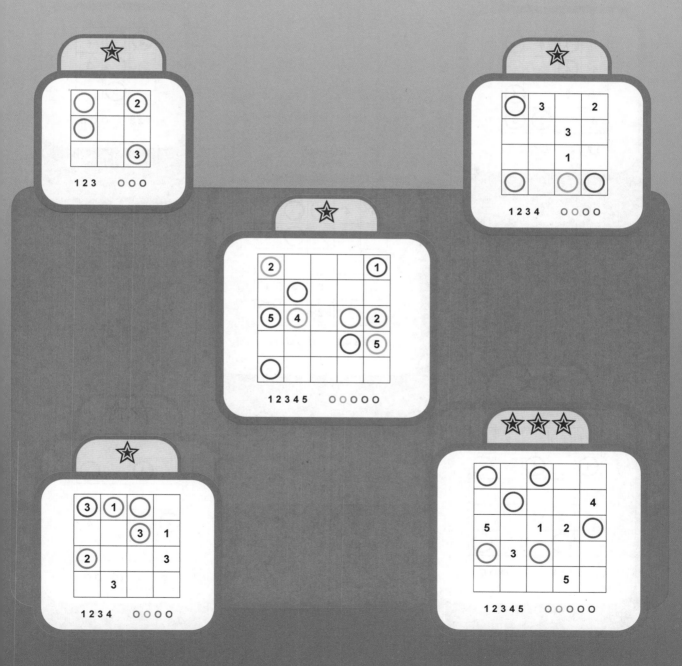

Turn to page 60 for the solutions **37**

	3	4	○
1	4		
3	2		4
4		2	3

1 2 3 4   ○ ○ ○ ○

3	○	2
	○	3
	3	

1 2 3   ○ ○ ○

5	4	○	○	
			○	2
		5	3	1
		2		○

1 2 3 4 5   ○ ○ ○ ○ ○

	○		2	
1		4		○
3	2	5		
	○			○

1 2 3 4 5   ○ ○ ○ ○ ○

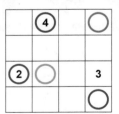

	4		○
2	○		3
			○

1 2 3 4   ○ ○ ○ ○

COMBIKU

Each horizontal row and vertical column should contain different colors and different numbers. Every square will contain one number and one colored circle and no combination may be repeated anywhere in the puzzle; so, for instance, if a square contains a 3 surrounded by a red circle, then no other square containing a 3 will have a red circle and no other square with a red circle will contain a 3.

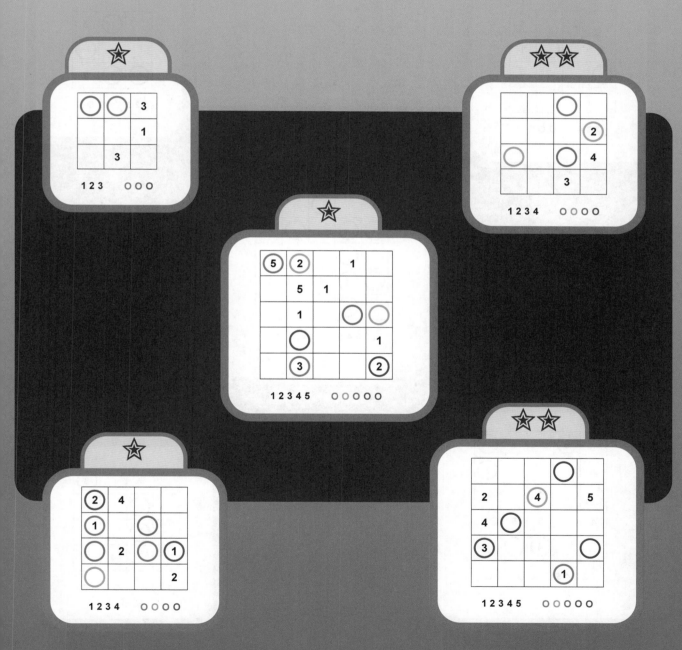

Turn to page 61 for the solutions **39**

1 2 3 4   ○○○○

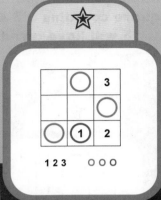

1 2 3   ○○○

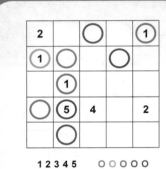

1 2 3 4 5   ○○○○○

1 2 3 4 5   ○○○○○

1 2 3 4   ○○○○

COMBIKU

Each horizontal row and vertical column should contain different colors and different numbers. Every square will contain one number and one colored circle and no combination may be repeated anywhere in the puzzle; so, for instance, if a square contains a 3 surrounded by a red circle, then no other square containing a 3 will have a red circle and no other square with a red circle will contain a 3.

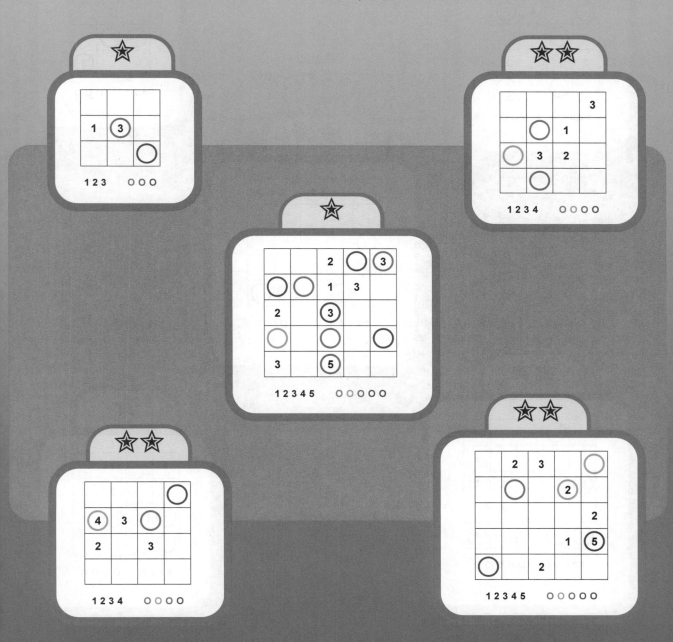

Turn to page 61 for the solutions **41**

COMBIKU

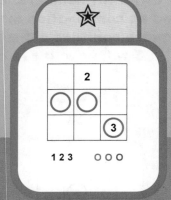

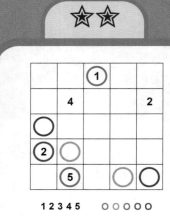

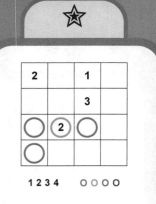

42 Turn to page 61 for the solutions

MAGIC SQUARE

Fill the square with the following numbers so that each line across, down and diagonally adds up to 51.

13, 14, 15, 16, 17, 18, 19, 20, 21

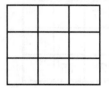

Fill the square with the following numbers so that each line across, down and diagonally adds up to 34. Some numbers are already in place.

2, 4, 8, 9, 10, 13, 14, 15, 16

	11	5	
			3
12	1		6
7			

Fill the square with the following numbers so that each line across, down and diagonally adds up to 48.

11, 12, 13, 15, 16, 17, 19, 20, 21

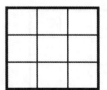

The numbers in each line of five squares across, down and diagonally should add up to 65, but in every row across and column down there is one number out of place. Swap these with one another to make the total correct.

8	9	24	17	15
2	25	18	11	10
21	19	12	14	3
20	13	1	4	22
6	7	5	23	16

Turn to page 62 for the solutions **43**

MAGIC SQUARE

Fill the square with the following numbers so that each line across, down and diagonally adds up to 15.

1, 3, 3, 5, 5, 5, 7, 7, 9

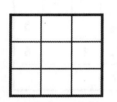

Fill the empty squares with numbers so that each line across, down and diagonally adds up to 72.

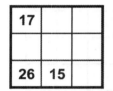

17		
26	15	

Fill the square with the following numbers so that each line across, down and diagonally adds up to 105.

25, 28, 31, 32, 35, 38, 39, 42, 45

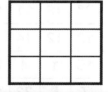

Fill the square with the following numbers so that each line across, down and diagonally adds up to 18.

2, 3, 4, 5, 6, 7, 8, 9, 10

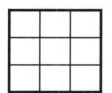

Fill the blank squares in the grid with the following numbers so that each line across, down and diagonally adds up to the totals shown. Every listed number is used just once.

**0, 1, 2, 3, 4,
5, 6, 7, 8, 9**

	6			=	25
	6			=	16
9	5		2	=	16
7				=	23

| = | = | = | = | = | = |
| 19 | 30 | 22 | 12 | 16 | 23 |

Fill the square with the following numbers so that each line across, down and diagonally adds up to 21.

3, 4, 5, 6, 7, 8, 9, 10, 11

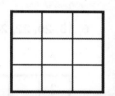

Fill the square with the following numbers so that each line across, down and diagonally adds up to 18.

1, 3, 4, 5, 6, 7, 8, 9, 11

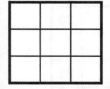

The numbers in each line of six squares across, down and diagonally should add up to 134, but in every row across and column down there is one number out of place. Swap these with one another to make the total correct.

20	24	17	17	25	42
37	22	13	20	24	21
13	29	22	18	12	19
15	39	34	26	10	20
12	10	26	34	32	31
16	21	32	22	17	12

Turn to page 62 for the solutions **45**

MAGIC SQUARE

Fill the square with the following numbers so that each line across, down and diagonally adds up to 68. Some numbers are already in place.

6, 18, 20, 22, 24, 26, 28, 30

2		16	
	14		4
	12		
8		10	32

Fill the square with the following numbers so that each line across, down and diagonally adds up to 15.

1, 2, 3, 4, 5, 6, 7, 8, 9

Fill the square with the following numbers so that each line across, down and diagonally adds up to 30.

2, 3, 4, 9, 10, 11, 16, 17, 18

Fill the square with the following numbers so that each line across, down and diagonally adds up to 99. Some numbers are already in place.

10, 16, 23, 23, 24, 28, 35, 37

22			38
	24		
31			21
9		25	30

MAGIC SQUARE

Fill the square with the following numbers so that each line across, down and diagonally adds up to 21.

2, 4, 5, 6, 7, 8, 9, 10, 12

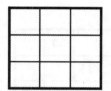

Fill the square with the following numbers so that each line across, down and diagonally adds up to 134. Some numbers are already in place.

17, 22, 24, 26, 27, 31, 34, 39, 45

57			
	33		
	40	22	41
29		49	

Fill the square with the following numbers so that each line across, down and diagonally adds up to 65. Some numbers are already in place.

5, 6, 10, 12, 13, 14, 14, 15

		13	29
27		18	
19		20	
	28		17

Fill the square with the following numbers so that each line across, down and diagonally adds up to 36.

7, 9, 10, 11, 12, 13, 14, 15, 17

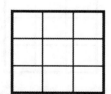

Turn to page 62 for the solutions

MAGIC SQUARE

Fill the square with the following numbers so that each line across, down and diagonally adds up to 34. Some numbers are already in place.

1, 2, 6, 7, 9, 10, 13, 14, 16

	12	8	
		11	
15			3
4		5	

Fill the square with the following numbers so that each line across, down and diagonally adds up to 99. Some numbers are already in place.

14, 17, 18, 19, 21, 25, 26, 27, 28, 41

		31	
13	34		
			42
	20	20	

Fill the square with the following numbers so that each line across, down and diagonally adds up to 30.

2, 4, 6, 8, 10, 12, 14, 16, 18

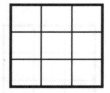

Fill the blank squares in the grid with the following numbers so that each line across, down and diagonally adds up to the totals shown. Every listed number is used just once.

**0, 1, 2, 3, 4,
5, 6, 7, 8, 9**

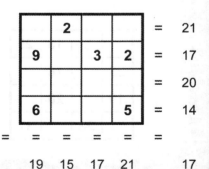

MAGIC SQUARE

Fill the square with the following numbers so that each line across, down and diagonally adds up to 43. Some numbers are already in place.

4, 6, 7, 9, 11, 12, 13, 15, 15

14			16
		13	10
14			
2			11

Fill the square with the following numbers so that each line across, down and diagonally adds up to 50. Some numbers are already in place.

8, 11, 11, 13, 13, 13, 13, 14, 14, 18, 19

			12
7			
		10	
16			8

Fill the square with the following numbers so that each line across, down and diagonally adds up to 67. Some numbers are already in place.

7, 10, 13, 13, 14, 17, 18, 19, 19, 21, 21, 22, 22, 24, 35

		3		
5	5			1
		5		
7			13	
14		3	4	

Fill the square with the following numbers so that each line across, down and diagonally adds up to 51. Some numbers are already in place.

3, 9, 12, 13, 14, 15, 16, 17, 21

	8		6
10			
		11	24
	18		7

Turn to page 63 for the solutions

HEXAGONY

Can you place the hexagons into the grid so that where any hexagon touches another along a straight line the contents of both triangles are the same? No rotation of any hexagon is allowed!

HEXAGONY

Turn to page 63 for the solutions

HEXAGONY

Can you place the hexagons into the grid so that where any hexagon touches another along a straight line the contents of both triangles are the same? No rotation of any hexagon is allowed!

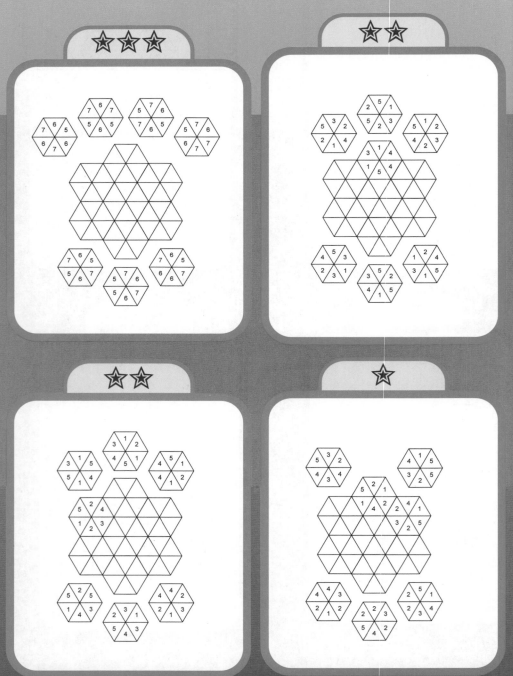

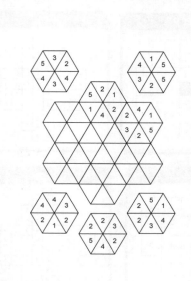

Turn to page 64 for the solutions

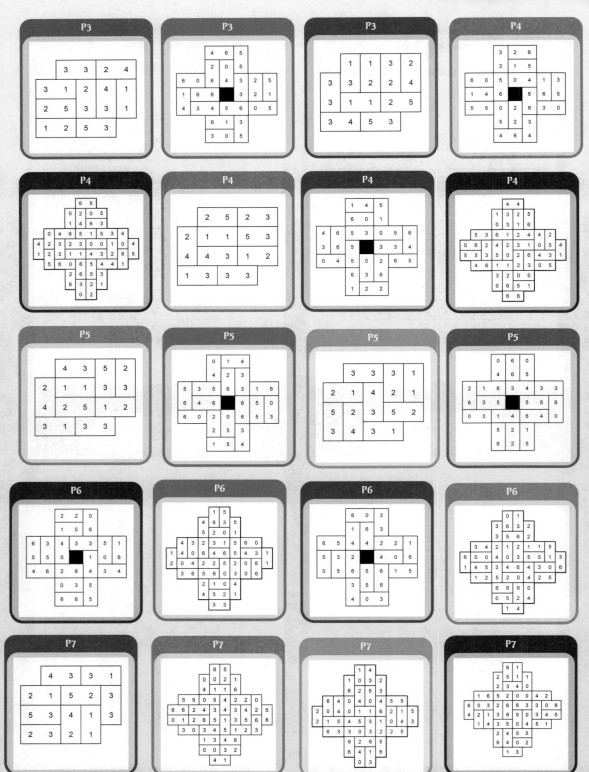

SOLUTIONS

SOLUTIONS

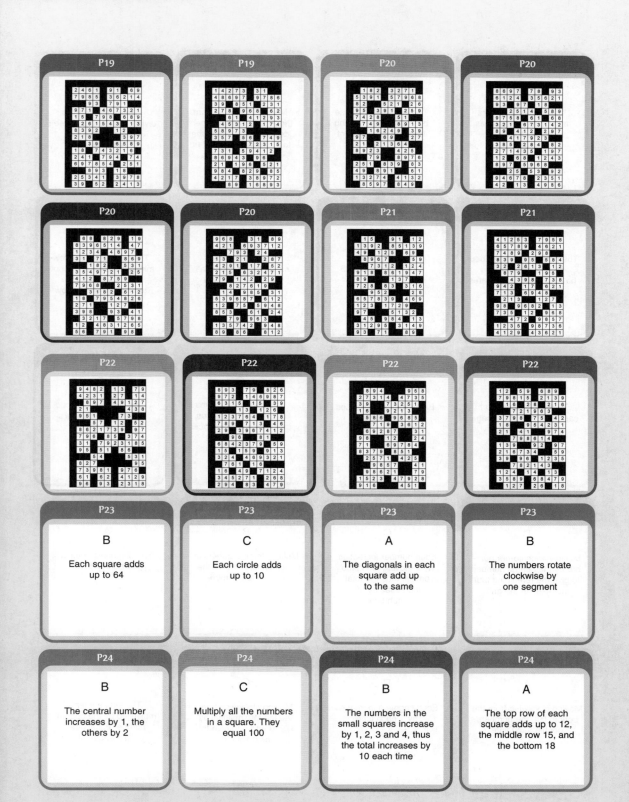

P19

P19

P20

P20

P20

P20

P21

P21

P22

P22

P22

P22

P23

B

Each square adds
up to 64

P23

C

Each circle adds
up to 10

P23

A

The diagonals in each
square add up
to the same

P23

B

The numbers rotate
clockwise by
one segment

P24

B

The central number
increases by 1, the
others by 2

P24

C

Multiply all the numbers
in a square. They
equal 100

P24

B

The numbers in the
small squares increase
by 1, 2, 3 and 4, thus
the total increases by
10 each time

P24

A

The top row of each
square adds up to 12,
the middle row 15, and
the bottom 18

P25

C

The top two numbers add up to the same as the bottom two

P25

A

The numbers increase by 2 clockwise starting from the left segment

P25

B

Moving clockwise from the top right the numbers decrease by 7, thus the top two numbers add up to the same as the bottom two

P25

B

The right segment divided by the bottom segment equals the left segment

P26

C

The odd numbers are doubled, even numbers halved, along the squares

P26

A

The total of the segments equals 25

P26

A

The digits of the numbers in each small square add up to 8

P26

A

The total of the top row minus the total of the bottom row equals the total of the middle row

P27

A

In each square you can add three of the segments together to give the fourth

P27

C

Each number increases by 5 each time

P27

C

The number 6 moves clockwise two spaces, the 4 moves four spaces and the 3 moves clockwise one

P27

B

The number 4 can go into all the numbers exactly

P28

D

Multiply each corner number by the central number to give the remaining four numbers in the grid

P28

C

Each number increases by 9 moving along the boxes, thus the total increases by 36 each time

P28

B

Multiply three numbers in each square to give the bottom left number

P28

A

The diagonals in each grid add up to 20

P29

A

Moving clockwise from the bottom left, the numbers double each time

P29

B

Each segment increases by 1 each time

P29

C

Moving clockwise from the top left, multiply by 1, 2, 3 and 4 to give the next square

P29

A

The left segment multiplied by the bottom number equals the right segment

SOLUTIONS

P30	P30	P30	P30
D	**A**	**B**	**D**
In each column subtract the second number from the top one to give the bottom number	Each number moves anti-clockwise by one place each time	When each column pair is multiplied the two left numbers equal the two right ones	The outer numbers all move clockwise round the grid two spaces

P31	P31	P31	P31
C	**A**	**B**	**C**
Each grid adds up to 15, 30, 45 then 60	The numbers decrease by 3 each time	One pair of diagonal numbers, when added, is six times larger than the sum of the other pair	Each circle equals 12 when the segments are multiplied

P32	P32	P32	P32
B	**B**	**D**	**C**
The corner numbers add up to the same as the other numbers	In every vertical column the numbers add up to 47	Each shape makes a one-sixth turn clockwise every time	All the numbers in the grid begin with the same letter when written

P33

3	2	1
2	1	3
1	3	2

P33

2	1	3	4
3	4	2	1
4	3	1	2
1	2	4	3

P33

5	4	3	2	1
2	3	1	4	5
3	5	2	1	4
4	1	5	3	2
1	2	4	5	3

P33

4	2	3	1
3	1	4	2
2	4	1	3
1	3	2	4

P33

2	5	4	1	3
5	1	3	4	2
1	4	2	3	5
4	3	5	2	1
3	2	1	5	4

P34

2	4	1	3
1	3	2	4
4	2	3	1
3	1	4	2

P34

2	1	3
3	2	1
1	3	2

P34

5	2	4	3	1
2	3	1	4	5
4	1	2	5	3
1	5	3	2	4
3	4	5	1	2

SOLUTIONS

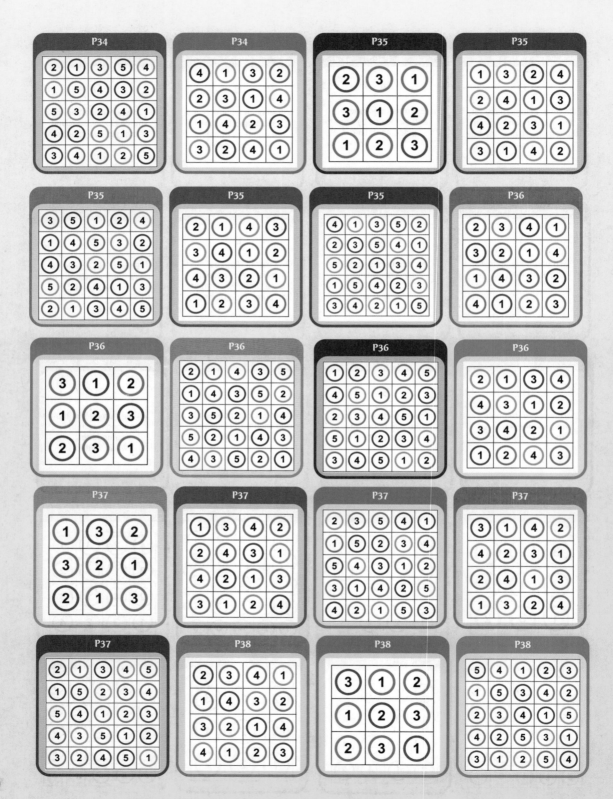

SOLUTIONS

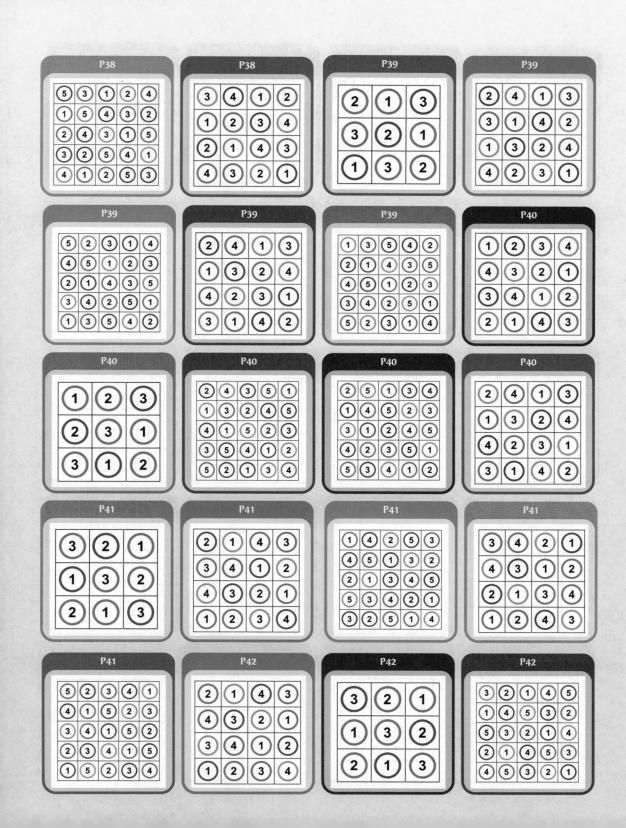

P42

P42

P43

Allowing for reflections and reversals, here is one possible solution:

14	19	18
21	17	13
16	15	20

P43

2	11	5	16
13	8	10	3
12	1	15	6
7	14	4	9

P43

Allowing for reflections and reversals, here is one possible solution:

12	21	15
19	16	13
17	11	20

P43

The numbers which have changed places are shown in bold type.

8	**1**	24	17	15
2	25	18	11	**9**
21	19	12	**10**	3
20	13	**6**	4	22
14	7	5	23	16

P44

Allowing for reflections and reversals, here is one possible solution:

3	9	3
5	5	5
7	1	7

P44

17	33	22
29	24	19
26	15	31

P44

Allowing for reflections and reversals, here is one possible solution:

38	39	28
25	35	45
42	31	32

P44

Allowing for reflections and reversals, here is one possible solution:

7	2	9
8	6	4
3	10	5

P45

8	6	7	4
6	6	3	1
9	5	0	2
7	5	2	9

P45

Allowing for reflections and reversals, here is one possible solution:

8	9	4
3	7	11
10	5	6

P45

Allowing for reflections and reversals, here is one possible solution:

3	7	8
11	6	1
4	5	9

P45

The numbers which have changed places are shown in bold type.

20	**13**	17	17	25	42
37	22	13	**17**	24	21
34	29	22	18	12	19
15	39	**24**	26	10	20
12	10	26	34	32	**20**
16	21	32	22	**31**	12

P46

2	24	16	26
28	14	22	4
30	12	20	6
8	18	10	32

P46

Allowing for reflections and reversals, here is one possible solution:

6	1	8
7	5	3
2	9	4

P46

Allowing for reflections and reversals, here is one possible solution:

3	18	9
16	10	4
11	2	17

P46

22	16	23	38
37	24	28	10
31	24	23	21
9	35	25	30

P47

Allowing for reflections and reversals, here is one possible solution:

4	8	9
12	7	2
5	6	10

P47

57	27	24	26
17	33	39	45
31	40	22	41
29	34	49	22

SOLUTIONS

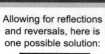

P47		

Allowing for reflections and reversals, here is one possible solution:

4	8	9
12	7	2
5	6	10

P47			
57	27	24	26
17	33	39	45
31	40	22	41
29	34	49	22

P48			
1	12	8	13
14	7	11	2
15	6	10	3
4	9	5	16

P48			
26	28	31	14
13	34	27	25
19	17	21	42
41	20	20	18

P48		

Allowing for reflections and reversals, here is one possible solution:

4	18	8
14	10	6
12	2	16

P48			
4	2	7	8
9	3	3	2
0	9	5	6
6	1	2	5

P49			
14	9	4	16
13	7	13	10
14	12	11	6
2	15	15	11

P49			
14	11	13	12
7	18	14	11
13	8	10	19
16	13	13	8

P49				
22	18	3	10	14
5	5	35	21	1
19	7	5	19	17
7	13	21	13	13
14	24	3	4	22

P49			
21	8	16	6
10	12	15	14
3	13	11	24
17	18	9	7

P50
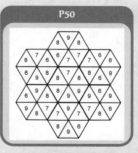

P50
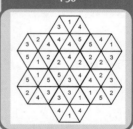

P50
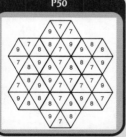

P50
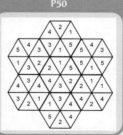

P51
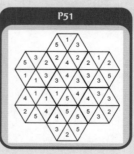

P51
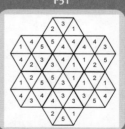

P51
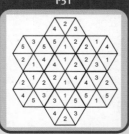

P51
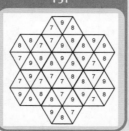